50 Healthy Breakfast Recipes for Home

By: Kelly Johnson

Table of Contents

- Greek Yogurt and Berry Parfait
- Spinach and Feta Egg Muffins
- Avocado Toast with Cherry Tomatoes
- Quinoa and Black Bean Salad
- Veggie-Packed Breakfast Burritos
- Smoked Salmon and Cream Cheese on Whole Grain Bagels
- Sweet Potato Hash with Poached Eggs
- Chia Seed Pudding with Almond Milk
- Kale and Mushroom Frittata
- Oatmeal with Fresh Fruit and Nuts
- Whole Wheat Banana Pancakes
- Veggie-Stuffed Omelette
- Almond Butter and Banana Smoothie
- Sweet Potato and Avocado Breakfast Tacos
- Cottage Cheese with Pineapple and Almonds
- Roasted Veggie and Hummus Wrap
- Green Smoothie with Spinach and Apple
- Zucchini Noodles with Pesto
- Berry and Spinach Smoothie Bowl
- Whole Grain Waffles with Berries
- Avocado and Egg Breakfast Bowl
- Turkey and Spinach Breakfast Casserole
- Fruit and Nut Overnight Oats
- Cauliflower Rice Stir-Fry with Eggs
- Greek Salad with Chicken
- Baked Apples with Cinnamon and Walnuts
- Chickpea and Spinach Stuffed Pita
- Almond Flour Muffins with Blueberries
- Veggie-Packed Quiche with a Sweet Potato Crust
- Peanut Butter and Strawberry Chia Jam Sandwich
- Egg and Avocado Breakfast Quesadilla
- Mediterranean Breakfast Bowl with Quinoa

- Cucumber and Hummus Sandwiches
- Spicy Black Bean and Sweet Potato Tacos
- Carrot and Zucchini Fritters
- Smoked Salmon and Avocado Salad
- Edamame and Corn Salad
- Protein-Packed Breakfast Smoothie with Spinach
- Whole Grain French Toast with Fresh Berries
- Apple and Walnut Oat Muffins
- Sweet Potato and Black Bean Enchiladas
- Baked Eggplant with Tomato and Basil
- Fresh Fruit Salad with Mint
- Smashed Chickpea and Avocado Toast
- Low-Carb Greek Chicken Skewers
- Tofu and Veggie Stir-Fry
- Pumpkin Spice Overnight Oats
- Pita Bread with Spinach and Feta
- Almond-Crusted Baked Chicken Tenders
- Butternut Squash and Kale Salad

Greek Yogurt and Berry Parfait

1. **Ingredients**: Greek yogurt, fresh berries (such as strawberries, blueberries, or raspberries), granola, and honey or maple syrup.
2. **Instructions**:
    - Layer Greek yogurt at the bottom of a glass or bowl.
    - Add a layer of fresh berries.
    - Sprinkle granola on top of the berries.
    - Drizzle with honey or maple syrup if desired.
    - Repeat layers until the glass or bowl is filled.
    - Top with a final sprinkle of granola and a few more berries.

Enjoy your delicious and healthy breakfast!

Spinach and Feta Egg Muffins

1. **Ingredients**: Eggs, fresh spinach (chopped), feta cheese (crumbled), salt, pepper, and optional herbs (like dill or parsley).
2. **Instructions**:
    - Preheat oven to 375°F (190°C) and grease a muffin tin.
    - In a bowl, whisk together eggs, salt, and pepper.
    - Stir in chopped spinach and crumbled feta.
    - Pour the mixture evenly into the muffin tin cups.
    - Bake for 15-20 minutes, or until eggs are set and tops are slightly golden.
    - Let cool slightly before serving.

Enjoy these savory, protein-packed muffins!

Avocado Toast with Cherry Tomatoes

Ingredients:

- 1 ripe avocado
- 2 slices of whole-grain bread
- 1 cup cherry tomatoes, halved
- 1 tablespoon olive oil
- Salt and pepper, to taste
- Fresh basil or cilantro, for garnish
- Red pepper flakes (optional)

Instructions:

1. Toast the bread slices to your desired crispiness.
2. Mash the avocado in a bowl, then season with salt and pepper.
3. Spread the mashed avocado evenly over the toasted bread.
4. Arrange the cherry tomato halves on top of the avocado.
5. Drizzle with olive oil and season with additional salt and pepper.
6. Garnish with fresh basil or cilantro and a pinch of red pepper flakes if you like a bit of heat.
7. Serve immediately and enjoy your flavorful, nutritious toast!

Quinoa and Black Bean Salad

Ingredients:

- 1 cup quinoa
- 2 cups water or vegetable broth
- 1 can (15 oz) black beans, drained and rinsed
- 1 cup corn kernels (fresh, frozen, or canned)
- 1 red bell pepper, diced
- 1/2 cup red onion, finely chopped
- 1 avocado, diced
- 1/4 cup fresh cilantro, chopped
- Juice of 1 lime
- 2 tablespoons olive oil
- Salt and pepper, to taste
- Optional: 1/2 teaspoon cumin or chili powder for extra flavor

Instructions:

1. **Cook the Quinoa:** Rinse the quinoa under cold water. In a medium saucepan, combine quinoa and water (or vegetable broth). Bring to a boil, then reduce heat to low, cover, and simmer for about 15 minutes, or until the quinoa is cooked and the liquid is absorbed. Remove from heat and let it sit, covered, for 5 minutes. Fluff with a fork and let it cool.
2. **Prepare the Vegetables:** While the quinoa is cooling, prepare the other ingredients. Dice the red bell pepper, chop the red onion, and dice the avocado. If using frozen corn, thaw it by running it under warm water or microwaving it for a minute or two.
3. **Combine the Ingredients:** In a large bowl, combine the cooked quinoa, black beans, corn, red bell pepper, red onion, and avocado.
4. **Make the Dressing:** In a small bowl, whisk together the lime juice, olive oil, salt, pepper, and optional cumin or chili powder if using.
5. **Toss and Serve:** Pour the dressing over the salad and gently toss to combine. Add the chopped cilantro and toss again.
6. **Chill (Optional):** For best flavors, let the salad chill in the refrigerator for at least 30 minutes before serving.

Enjoy this salad as a light main course or a flavorful side dish!

Veggie-Packed Breakfast Burritos

Ingredients:

- **For the Burritos:**
    - 1 tablespoon olive oil
    - 1 small onion, diced
    - 1 bell pepper (any color), diced
    - 1 cup mushrooms, sliced
    - 1 cup spinach or kale, chopped
    - 1 medium tomato, diced
    - 1 can (15 oz) black beans, drained and rinsed
    - 1 cup shredded cheddar cheese (or your preferred cheese)
    - 4 large eggs
    - 4 large tortillas (whole wheat or flour)
- **For the Optional Garnishes:**
    - Salsa
    - Avocado slices or guacamole
    - Sour cream or Greek yogurt
    - Hot sauce

Instructions:

1. **Prepare the Vegetables:**
    - Heat the olive oil in a large skillet over medium heat.
    - Add the diced onion and bell pepper, and cook for about 3-4 minutes until they start to soften.
    - Add the sliced mushrooms and cook for an additional 3 minutes until they begin to brown.
    - Stir in the chopped spinach or kale and cook until wilted, about 1-2 minutes.
    - Add the diced tomato and black beans, and cook for another 2 minutes until heated through. Season with salt and pepper to taste. Remove the vegetable mixture from the skillet and set aside.
2. **Cook the Eggs:**
    - In the same skillet, scramble the eggs. You can cook them in a bit of butter or oil if you prefer. Season with salt and pepper.
    - Once the eggs are cooked, fold them into the vegetable mixture. Stir in the shredded cheese until it melts and everything is well combined.
3. **Assemble the Burritos:**
    - Warm the tortillas in a dry skillet or microwave for a few seconds to make them more pliable.
    - Place a portion of the veggie-egg mixture in the center of each tortilla.
    - Fold in the sides and then roll up the burrito from the bottom, tucking in the sides as you go to enclose the filling.

4. **Serve:**
    - Optionally, you can heat the burritos in a skillet for a minute or two on each side to get a crispy exterior.
    - Serve with your choice of garnishes such as salsa, avocado slices or guacamole, sour cream or Greek yogurt, and hot sauce.

Enjoy your veggie-packed breakfast burritos as a delicious start to your day or as a make-ahead meal for busy mornings!

Smoked Salmon and Cream Cheese on Whole Grain Bagels

Ingredients:

- 2 whole grain bagels
- 4 oz cream cheese, softened
- 4 oz smoked salmon, sliced
- 1/4 small red onion, thinly sliced
- 1/2 cucumber, thinly sliced
- Capers (optional)
- Fresh dill or chives (optional)
- Lemon wedges (optional)

Instructions:

1. **Toast the Bagels:** Slice the bagels in half and toast them to your preference.
2. **Spread Cream Cheese:** Evenly spread a layer of cream cheese on each toasted bagel half.
3. **Add Salmon:** Place slices of smoked salmon on top of the cream cheese.
4. **Add Toppings:** Arrange the thinly sliced red onion and cucumber over the salmon. Add capers and fresh dill or chives if desired.
5. **Serve:** Optionally, serve with lemon wedges on the side for a fresh squeeze of citrus.

Enjoy your delicious and satisfying bagel!

Sweet Potato Hash with Poached Eggs

Ingredients:

- 2 large sweet potatoes, peeled and diced
- 1 tablespoon olive oil
- 1 small onion, diced
- 1 red bell pepper, diced
- 1 cup spinach or kale, chopped
- 1 teaspoon smoked paprika
- Salt and pepper, to taste
- 4 large eggs
- 1 tablespoon vinegar (for poaching)
- Fresh herbs (optional), for garnish

Instructions:

1. **Cook the Sweet Potatoes:** Heat olive oil in a large skillet over medium heat. Add diced sweet potatoes and cook, stirring occasionally, until they start to soften, about 10 minutes.
2. **Add Vegetables:** Add the onion and red bell pepper to the skillet. Cook for another 5 minutes, or until vegetables are tender and slightly caramelized. Stir in the spinach or kale until wilted. Season with smoked paprika, salt, and pepper.
3. **Poach the Eggs:** Fill a medium saucepan with water and add vinegar. Bring to a simmer. Crack each egg into a small bowl, then gently slide into the simmering water. Poach eggs for 3-4 minutes, until whites are set but yolks are still runny. Remove with a slotted spoon and drain.
4. **Assemble:** Divide the sweet potato hash among plates. Top each serving with a poached egg.
5. **Garnish:** Optionally, garnish with fresh herbs.

Enjoy this hearty and flavorful breakfast!

Chia Seed Pudding with Almond Milk

Ingredients:

- 1/4 cup chia seeds
- 1 cup almond milk (unsweetened or sweetened)
- 1-2 tablespoons maple syrup or honey (to taste)
- 1/2 teaspoon vanilla extract
- Fresh fruit or nuts (optional, for topping)

Instructions:

1. **Mix Ingredients:** In a bowl or jar, combine chia seeds, almond milk, maple syrup (or honey), and vanilla extract. Stir well to mix.
2. **Refrigerate:** Cover and refrigerate for at least 4 hours or overnight, allowing the chia seeds to absorb the liquid and thicken.
3. **Serve:** Stir the pudding before serving. Top with fresh fruit, nuts, or any other toppings you like.

Enjoy your creamy, nutritious chia seed pudding!

Kale and Mushroom Frittata

Ingredients:

- 1 tablespoon olive oil
- 1 cup mushrooms, sliced
- 1 cup kale, chopped
- 6 large eggs
- 1/4 cup milk or cream
- 1/2 cup shredded cheese (e.g., cheddar, feta, or goat cheese)
- Salt and pepper, to taste
- 1/4 teaspoon garlic powder (optional)

Instructions:

1. **Preheat Oven:** Preheat your oven to 375°F (190°C).
2. **Cook Vegetables:** Heat olive oil in an oven-safe skillet over medium heat. Add mushrooms and cook until they start to soften, about 5 minutes. Add kale and cook until wilted, about 2 minutes. Season with salt, pepper, and garlic powder if using.
3. **Prepare Egg Mixture:** In a bowl, whisk together eggs, milk or cream, and cheese. Season with a pinch of salt and pepper.
4. **Combine and Cook:** Pour the egg mixture over the vegetables in the skillet. Stir gently to distribute evenly. Cook on the stovetop for 2-3 minutes until the edges start to set.
5. **Bake:** Transfer the skillet to the preheated oven and bake for 15-20 minutes, or until the frittata is fully set and lightly golden on top.
6. **Cool and Serve:** Let it cool for a few minutes before slicing and serving.

Enjoy your delicious kale and mushroom frittata!

Oatmeal with Fresh Fruit and Nuts

Ingredients:

- 1 cup rolled oats
- 2 cups water or milk (dairy or non-dairy)
- 1/2 teaspoon cinnamon (optional)
- 1 tablespoon honey or maple syrup (optional)
- Fresh fruit of your choice (e.g., berries, apple slices, banana)
- Nuts of your choice (e.g., almonds, walnuts, pecans), chopped
- A pinch of salt

Instructions:

1. **Cook the Oats:**
    - In a medium saucepan, bring water or milk to a boil.
    - Add a pinch of salt and the rolled oats.
    - Reduce heat to low and simmer, stirring occasionally, for about 5-7 minutes, or until the oats are tender and have absorbed most of the liquid.
    - If using cinnamon and/or sweetener, stir them in during the last minute of cooking.
2. **Prepare the Toppings:**
    - While the oats are cooking, prepare your fresh fruit by washing and slicing it as needed.
    - Chop your nuts if they're not pre-chopped.
3. **Serve:**
    - Spoon the cooked oatmeal into bowls.
    - Top with fresh fruit and nuts.
    - Add a drizzle of honey or maple syrup if desired.

Feel free to mix and match fruits and nuts based on what you have on hand or your personal preferences. Enjoy your nutritious and delicious oatmeal!

Whole Wheat Banana Pancakes

Ingredients:

- 1 cup whole wheat flour
- 1 tablespoon baking powder
- 1/2 teaspoon salt
- 1 tablespoon honey or maple syrup
- 1 cup milk (dairy or non-dairy)
- 1 large egg
- 1 ripe banana, mashed
- 1 teaspoon vanilla extract
- 1 tablespoon olive oil or melted butter (for cooking)

Instructions:

1. **Mix Dry Ingredients:** In a bowl, whisk together whole wheat flour, baking powder, and salt.
2. **Combine Wet Ingredients:** In another bowl, mix honey or maple syrup, milk, egg, mashed banana, and vanilla extract.
3. **Combine Mixtures:** Pour the wet ingredients into the dry ingredients and stir until just combined. The batter may be slightly lumpy, which is fine.
4. **Cook Pancakes:** Heat a skillet or griddle over medium heat and lightly coat with olive oil or melted butter. Pour 1/4 cup of batter for each pancake onto the skillet. Cook until bubbles form on the surface, then flip and cook until golden brown on the other side.
5. **Serve:** Serve warm with your favorite toppings like fresh fruit, yogurt, or a drizzle of honey or maple syrup.

Enjoy your wholesome banana pancakes!

Veggie-Stuffed Omelette

Ingredients:

- 3 large eggs
- 1 tablespoon olive oil or butter
- 1/4 cup onion, diced
- 1/2 cup bell peppers, diced
- 1/2 cup mushrooms, sliced
- 1/2 cup spinach or kale, chopped
- 1/4 cup shredded cheese (e.g., cheddar, feta, or goat cheese)
- Salt and pepper, to taste

Instructions:

1. **Prepare Vegetables:** Heat olive oil or butter in a non-stick skillet over medium heat. Add onions and bell peppers, cooking until softened, about 3-4 minutes. Add mushrooms and cook until tender, about 2 minutes more. Stir in spinach or kale until wilted. Season with salt and pepper.
2. **Cook Eggs:** In a bowl, whisk the eggs with a pinch of salt and pepper. Pour eggs into the skillet over the cooked vegetables. Cook until the edges start to set, then gently lift the edges with a spatula, tilting the pan to let uncooked egg flow to the edges.
3. **Add Cheese:** Once the eggs are mostly set, sprinkle cheese over half of the omelette. Let it melt for about 1 minute.
4. **Fold and Serve:** Carefully fold the omelette in half over the cheese. Cook for another 1-2 minutes until fully set and cheese is melted. Slide onto a plate and serve hot.

Enjoy your veggie-packed omelette!

Almond Butter and Banana Smoothie

Ingredients:

- 1 ripe banana
- 1 tablespoon almond butter
- 1 cup milk (dairy or non-dairy)
- 1/2 cup Greek yogurt or a splash of vanilla extract (optional for extra creaminess)
- 1 tablespoon honey or maple syrup (optional, for sweetness)
- A few ice cubes (optional, for a chilled smoothie)

Instructions:

1. **Blend Ingredients:** In a blender, combine the banana, almond butter, milk, and Greek yogurt or vanilla extract if using. Add honey or maple syrup if desired.
2. **Blend:** Blend until smooth and creamy. Add ice cubes if you prefer a colder, thicker texture and blend again.
3. **Serve:** Pour into a glass and enjoy immediately.

This smoothie is creamy, nutritious, and perfect for a quick breakfast or snack!

Sweet Potato and Avocado Breakfast Tacos

Ingredients:

- **For the Tacos:**
    - 1 medium sweet potato, peeled and diced
    - 1 tablespoon olive oil
    - 1/2 teaspoon paprika
    - 1/2 teaspoon cumin
    - Salt and pepper, to taste
    - 4 small tortillas (corn or flour)
    - 1 ripe avocado, sliced
    - 1/4 cup red onion, finely chopped
    - Fresh cilantro, chopped (for garnish)
    - Lime wedges (for serving)
- **Optional Toppings:**
    - Salsa or pico de gallo
    - Crumbled feta or shredded cheese
    - Hot sauce

Instructions:

1. **Cook Sweet Potatoes:**
    - Preheat your oven to 400°F (200°C) or heat a skillet over medium heat.
    - If using the oven, toss the diced sweet potatoes with olive oil, paprika, cumin, salt, and pepper. Spread them in a single layer on a baking sheet and roast for 20-25 minutes, or until tender and slightly caramelized, flipping halfway through.
    - If using a skillet, heat the olive oil over medium heat, add the sweet potatoes, and cook, stirring occasionally, for about 10-15 minutes, until tender and slightly crispy.
2. **Prepare Tortillas:**
    - Warm the tortillas in a dry skillet over medium heat for about 30 seconds on each side, or wrap them in foil and heat them in the oven for 5-7 minutes.
3. **Assemble Tacos:**
    - Spread a few slices of avocado on each tortilla.
    - Add a generous scoop of roasted sweet potatoes on top of the avocado.
    - Sprinkle with chopped red onion and fresh cilantro.
4. **Add Optional Toppings:**
    - Top with salsa or pico de gallo, crumbled feta or shredded cheese, and a dash of hot sauce if desired.
5. **Serve:**
    - Serve the tacos with lime wedges on the side for a squeeze of fresh lime juice.

Enjoy your flavorful and satisfying breakfast tacos!

Cottage Cheese with Pineapple and Almonds

Ingredients:

- 1 cup cottage cheese
- 1/2 cup fresh pineapple chunks (or canned, drained)
- 2 tablespoons sliced almonds
- 1 tablespoon honey or maple syrup (optional, for sweetness)

Instructions:

1. **Combine Ingredients:** In a bowl, mix together the cottage cheese and pineapple chunks.
2. **Add Almonds:** Sprinkle the sliced almonds on top.
3. **Sweeten (Optional):** Drizzle with honey or maple syrup if you like a touch of extra sweetness.
4. **Serve:** Enjoy immediately, or chill in the refrigerator for a refreshing snack.

This combination is both nutritious and delicious!

Roasted Veggie and Hummus Wrap

Ingredients:

- **For the Roasted Veggies:**
    - 1 red bell pepper, sliced
    - 1 zucchini, sliced
    - 1 small red onion, sliced
    - 1 cup cherry tomatoes, halved
    - 1 tablespoon olive oil
    - 1 teaspoon dried oregano
    - 1/2 teaspoon garlic powder
    - Salt and pepper, to taste
- **For the Wraps:**
    - 4 large whole wheat or flour tortillas
    - 1 cup hummus (store-bought or homemade)
    - Fresh spinach or arugula (optional)
    - Feta cheese or crumbled goat cheese (optional)

Instructions:

1. **Preheat Oven:** Preheat your oven to 400°F (200°C).
2. **Roast the Veggies:**
    - On a baking sheet, toss the sliced bell pepper, zucchini, red onion, and cherry tomatoes with olive oil, dried oregano, garlic powder, salt, and pepper.
    - Spread the vegetables in a single layer.
    - Roast for 20-25 minutes, or until the vegetables are tender and slightly caramelized, stirring halfway through.
3. **Prepare the Wraps:**
    - Warm the tortillas in a dry skillet over medium heat for about 30 seconds on each side or microwave them for a few seconds to make them more pliable.
    - Spread a generous layer of hummus on each tortilla.
4. **Assemble the Wraps:**
    - Once the vegetables are roasted and slightly cooled, evenly distribute them over the hummus-covered tortillas.
    - Add fresh spinach or arugula if using.
    - Sprinkle with feta cheese or crumbled goat cheese if desired.
5. **Roll and Serve:**
    - Roll up each tortilla tightly, then cut in half if desired.
    - Serve immediately or wrap in foil or parchment paper for a portable lunch.

Enjoy your flavorful and nutritious Roasted Veggie and Hummus Wrap!

Green Smoothie with Spinach and Apple

Ingredients:

- 1 cup fresh spinach
- 1 green apple, cored and chopped
- 1/2 banana (optional, for added creaminess)
- 1/2 cucumber, peeled and chopped
- 1 cup water or coconut water
- 1/2 cup ice (optional)
- 1 tablespoon lemon juice (optional, for extra freshness)
- 1 teaspoon honey or maple syrup (optional, for sweetness)

Instructions:

1. **Blend Ingredients:** In a blender, combine the spinach, apple, banana (if using), cucumber, and water or coconut water.
2. **Add Ice and Sweetener:** Add ice if you prefer a colder smoothie. Blend until smooth. Add lemon juice and honey or maple syrup if desired, and blend again briefly.
3. **Serve:** Pour into a glass and enjoy immediately for the best flavor and nutrient content.

This smoothie is packed with vitamins and makes for a great, invigorating start to your day!

Zucchini Noodles with Pesto

Ingredients:

- 2 medium zucchinis
- 1/4 cup pesto (store-bought or homemade)
- 1 tablespoon olive oil
- 1 tablespoon grated Parmesan cheese (optional)
- Cherry tomatoes, halved (optional)
- Pine nuts or walnuts, toasted (optional)

Instructions:

1. **Prepare Zucchini Noodles:** Use a spiralizer or vegetable peeler to turn the zucchinis into noodles. If using a peeler, make long, thin strips.
2. **Cook Noodles:** Heat olive oil in a skillet over medium heat. Add zucchini noodles and sauté for 2-3 minutes, just until they start to soften. Be careful not to overcook; they should remain slightly crisp.
3. **Toss with Pesto:** Remove from heat and toss the zucchini noodles with pesto until evenly coated.
4. **Serve:** Top with grated Parmesan cheese, cherry tomatoes, and toasted pine nuts or walnuts if desired.

Enjoy your fresh and vibrant zucchini noodles with pesto!

Berry and Spinach Smoothie Bowl

Ingredients:

- 1 cup fresh spinach
- 1 cup mixed berries (fresh or frozen; e.g., strawberries, blueberries, raspberries)
- 1/2 banana (fresh or frozen)
- 1/2 cup Greek yogurt or non-dairy yogurt
- 1/2 cup almond milk (or any milk of choice)
- 1 tablespoon honey or maple syrup (optional, for sweetness)

Toppings (optional):

- Sliced fresh berries
- Granola
- Chia seeds
- Nuts or seeds
- Coconut flakes

Instructions:

1. **Blend Smoothie:** In a blender, combine spinach, mixed berries, banana, yogurt, and almond milk. Blend until smooth. Adjust sweetness with honey or maple syrup if desired.
2. **Serve:** Pour the smoothie into a bowl.
3. **Add Toppings:** Decorate with your choice of toppings like sliced berries, granola, chia seeds, nuts, or coconut flakes.

Enjoy your nutritious and delicious smoothie bowl!

Whole Grain Waffles with Berries

Ingredients:

- **For the Waffles:**
    - 1 1/2 cups whole grain flour (e.g., whole wheat or spelt flour)
    - 1 tablespoon baking powder
    - 1/2 teaspoon salt
    - 2 tablespoons honey or maple syrup
    - 1 1/2 cups milk (dairy or non-dairy)
    - 2 large eggs
    - 1/4 cup melted coconut oil or butter
    - 1 teaspoon vanilla extract
- **For the Toppings:**
    - 1 cup mixed fresh berries (e.g., strawberries, blueberries, raspberries)
    - 1 tablespoon honey or maple syrup (optional, for drizzling)
    - A sprinkle of powdered sugar (optional)

Instructions:

1. **Preheat Waffle Maker:** Preheat your waffle maker according to the manufacturer's instructions.
2. **Prepare Waffle Batter:** In a large bowl, whisk together the whole grain flour, baking powder, and salt. In another bowl, mix honey or maple syrup, milk, eggs, melted coconut oil or butter, and vanilla extract. Pour the wet ingredients into the dry ingredients and stir until just combined.
3. **Cook Waffles:** Lightly grease the waffle maker. Pour the batter onto the preheated waffle iron and cook according to the manufacturer's instructions until golden brown and crispy.
4. **Prepare Toppings:** While the waffles are cooking, wash and slice the fresh berries.
5. **Serve:** Top the cooked waffles with fresh berries and a drizzle of honey or maple syrup if desired. Sprinkle with powdered sugar if using.

Enjoy your wholesome and delicious whole grain waffles with berries!

Avocado and Egg Breakfast Bowl

Ingredients:

- 1 ripe avocado
- 2 large eggs
- 1 tablespoon olive oil or butter
- 1/2 cup cooked quinoa or brown rice (optional, for extra heartiness)
- 1/4 cup cherry tomatoes, halved
- 1/4 cup fresh spinach or arugula
- Salt and pepper, to taste
- Red pepper flakes or hot sauce (optional)
- Fresh herbs (e.g., cilantro or chives), for garnish (optional)

Instructions:

1. **Cook the Eggs:**
   - **Poached Eggs:** Fill a saucepan with water and bring to a gentle simmer. Add a splash of vinegar if desired. Crack each egg into a small bowl and gently slide into the simmering water. Poach for 3-4 minutes until whites are set but yolks are still runny. Remove with a slotted spoon and set aside.
   - **Fried Eggs:** Heat olive oil or butter in a skillet over medium heat. Crack the eggs into the skillet and cook to your desired doneness (sunny side up, over-easy, etc.). Season with salt and pepper.
2. **Prepare the Bowl:**
   - **Base:** If using, add a layer of cooked quinoa or brown rice to the bottom of the bowl.
   - **Add Vegetables:** Top with fresh spinach or arugula and cherry tomatoes.
3. **Assemble:**
   - Slice the avocado and arrange it on top of the vegetables.
   - Place the cooked egg(s) on top of the avocado and vegetables.
4. **Season and Garnish:**
   - Season with salt, pepper, and red pepper flakes or hot sauce if desired.
   - Garnish with fresh herbs if using.

Enjoy your delicious and nutritious avocado and egg breakfast bowl!

Turkey and Spinach Breakfast Casserole

Ingredients:

- 1 tablespoon olive oil
- 1/2 pound ground turkey
- 1 small onion, diced
- 2 cups fresh spinach, chopped
- 6 large eggs
- 1/2 cup milk (dairy or non-dairy)
- 1 cup shredded cheese (e.g., cheddar or mozzarella)
- 1/2 teaspoon garlic powder
- 1/2 teaspoon dried oregano
- Salt and pepper, to taste

Instructions:

1. **Preheat Oven:** Preheat your oven to 375°F (190°C).
2. **Cook Turkey:** Heat olive oil in a skillet over medium heat. Add ground turkey and cook until browned, breaking it up with a spoon. Add diced onion and cook until translucent. Stir in chopped spinach and cook until wilted. Season with garlic powder, oregano, salt, and pepper.
3. **Prepare Egg Mixture:** In a large bowl, whisk together eggs and milk. Stir in shredded cheese.
4. **Combine and Bake:** Spread the cooked turkey and spinach mixture evenly in a greased baking dish. Pour the egg mixture over the top. Stir gently to combine.
5. **Bake:** Bake in the preheated oven for 25-30 minutes, or until the casserole is set and the top is lightly golden.
6. **Cool and Serve:** Let the casserole cool slightly before slicing. Enjoy warm.

This breakfast casserole is perfect for meal prepping and can be served for a delicious start to your day!

Fruit and Nut Overnight Oats

Ingredients:

- 1/2 cup rolled oats
- 1/2 cup milk (dairy or non-dairy)
- 1/2 cup Greek yogurt or a splash of vanilla extract (optional for extra creaminess)
- 1 tablespoon chia seeds (optional, for added texture and nutrition)
- 1 tablespoon honey or maple syrup (or to taste)
- 1/2 teaspoon vanilla extract (optional)
- Fresh fruit of your choice (e.g., berries, banana, apple)
- Nuts of your choice (e.g., almonds, walnuts, pecans), chopped

Instructions:

1. **Combine Ingredients:** In a jar or airtight container, mix together the rolled oats, milk, Greek yogurt (if using), chia seeds (if using), honey or maple syrup, and vanilla extract.
2. **Stir and Refrigerate:** Stir the mixture well to combine. Seal the container and refrigerate overnight (or for at least 4 hours) to let the oats absorb the liquid and soften.
3. **Add Toppings:** In the morning, give the oats a good stir. Top with fresh fruit and nuts.
4. **Serve:** Enjoy your overnight oats cold, or heat them up in the microwave if you prefer them warm.

Feel free to customize the recipe with your favorite fruits, nuts, or seeds!

Cauliflower Rice Stir-Fry with Eggs

Ingredients:

- 1 medium head of cauliflower
- 2 tablespoons olive oil or sesame oil
- 1 small onion, diced
- 2 cloves garlic, minced
- 1 cup mixed vegetables (e.g., bell peppers, carrots, peas)
- 2 large eggs
- 2 tablespoons soy sauce (or tamari for gluten-free)
- 1 teaspoon ginger, grated (optional)
- 2 green onions, sliced (for garnish)
- Sesame seeds (for garnish, optional)
- Fresh cilantro or parsley (for garnish, optional)

Instructions:

1. **Prepare Cauliflower Rice:**
    - Remove the leaves and stem from the cauliflower. Cut it into florets.
    - Use a food processor to pulse the cauliflower florets into rice-sized pieces. Alternatively, you can grate the cauliflower using a box grater.
2. **Cook the Vegetables:**
    - Heat 1 tablespoon of olive oil or sesame oil in a large skillet or wok over medium heat.
    - Add the diced onion and cook until translucent, about 3-4 minutes.
    - Add minced garlic and cook for another 30 seconds until fragrant.
    - Add mixed vegetables and cook until tender-crisp, about 5-7 minutes. If using ginger, add it here and cook for an additional minute.
3. **Add Cauliflower Rice:**
    - Push the vegetables to one side of the skillet. Add the remaining 1 tablespoon of oil to the empty side.
    - Add the cauliflower rice and cook, stirring occasionally, for about 5-7 minutes, until the cauliflower is tender but not mushy. Mix the vegetables and cauliflower rice together.
4. **Cook the Eggs:**
    - Push the cauliflower rice and vegetables to one side of the skillet. Crack the eggs into the empty side and scramble them, cooking until fully set.
    - Once the eggs are cooked, mix them into the cauliflower rice and vegetable mixture.
5. **Season and Serve:**
    - Stir in soy sauce and adjust seasoning with additional salt and pepper if needed.
    - Garnish with sliced green onions, sesame seeds, and fresh herbs if desired.

Enjoy your nutritious and delicious Cauliflower Rice Stir-Fry with Eggs!

Greek Salad with Chicken

Ingredients:

- **For the Salad:**
    - 2 cups cooked chicken breast, diced or sliced (grilled or baked)
    - 4 cups mixed greens or romaine lettuce, chopped
    - 1 cucumber, sliced
    - 1 cup cherry tomatoes, halved
    - 1/2 red onion, thinly sliced
    - 1/2 cup Kalamata olives, pitted
    - 1/2 cup crumbled feta cheese
    - 1/4 cup fresh parsley, chopped (optional)
- **For the Dressing:**
    - 1/4 cup extra-virgin olive oil
    - 2 tablespoons red wine vinegar
    - 1 teaspoon Dijon mustard
    - 1 clove garlic, minced
    - 1 teaspoon dried oregano
    - Salt and pepper, to taste

Instructions:

1. **Prepare the Chicken:**
    - If not already cooked, season chicken breasts with salt, pepper, and your choice of herbs or spices. Grill or bake until fully cooked. Let it rest for a few minutes before slicing or dicing.
2. **Prepare the Salad:**
    - In a large salad bowl, combine the mixed greens, cucumber, cherry tomatoes, red onion, olives, and feta cheese.
    - Add the cooked chicken on top of the salad.
3. **Make the Dressing:**
    - In a small bowl or jar, whisk together olive oil, red wine vinegar, Dijon mustard, minced garlic, dried oregano, salt, and pepper until well combined.
4. **Dress the Salad:**
    - Drizzle the dressing over the salad and toss gently to coat everything evenly.
5. **Garnish and Serve:**
    - Garnish with fresh parsley if desired.
    - Serve immediately, or chill in the refrigerator until ready to serve.

Enjoy your refreshing and protein-packed Greek Salad with Chicken!

Baked Apples with Cinnamon and Walnuts

Ingredients:

- 4 large apples (e.g., Honeycrisp, Granny Smith)
- 1/4 cup chopped walnuts
- 1/4 cup raisins or dried cranberries (optional)
- 2 tablespoons honey or maple syrup
- 1 teaspoon ground cinnamon
- 1/4 teaspoon ground nutmeg (optional)
- 1 tablespoon butter or coconut oil
- A pinch of salt

Instructions:

1. **Preheat Oven:** Preheat your oven to 350°F (175°C).
2. **Prepare Apples:** Core the apples, creating a cavity in the center. You can use an apple corer or a small knife.
3. **Mix Filling:** In a small bowl, combine chopped walnuts, raisins or dried cranberries (if using), honey or maple syrup, ground cinnamon, nutmeg (if using), and a pinch of salt. Mix well.
4. **Stuff Apples:** Place a small amount of butter or coconut oil in the bottom of each apple cavity, then spoon the walnut mixture into each apple, packing it in.
5. **Bake Apples:** Place the stuffed apples in a baking dish. Add a small amount of water (about 1/4 cup) to the bottom of the dish to help steam the apples. Bake in the preheated oven for 25-30 minutes, or until the apples are tender but still hold their shape.
6. **Serve:** Let the apples cool slightly before serving. They're great on their own or with a scoop of vanilla ice cream or a dollop of Greek yogurt.

Enjoy your warm and comforting baked apples!

Chickpea and Spinach Stuffed Pita

Ingredients:

- 1 can (15 oz) chickpeas, drained and rinsed
- 1 tablespoon olive oil
- 1 small onion, diced
- 2 cloves garlic, minced
- 1 teaspoon ground cumin
- 1/2 teaspoon paprika
- 1/2 teaspoon turmeric (optional)
- 2 cups fresh spinach, chopped
- 1/4 cup fresh parsley, chopped (optional)
- Salt and pepper, to taste
- 4 whole wheat pita pockets
- 1/2 cup plain Greek yogurt or tzatziki (optional, for serving)
- Lemon wedges (optional, for serving)

Instructions:

1. **Cook Chickpeas:**
    - Heat olive oil in a large skillet over medium heat.
    - Add diced onion and cook until translucent, about 3-4 minutes.
    - Add minced garlic and cook for another 30 seconds until fragrant.
    - Stir in ground cumin, paprika, and turmeric (if using). Cook for another minute.
2. **Add Chickpeas and Spinach:**
    - Add the drained chickpeas to the skillet. Cook, stirring occasionally, for about 5 minutes to allow the flavors to meld.
    - Add chopped spinach and cook until wilted, about 2-3 minutes.
    - Season with salt and pepper to taste. Stir in fresh parsley if using.
3. **Prepare Pita:**
    - Cut the whole wheat pita pockets in half to create pockets. If needed, warm the pita halves in a dry skillet over medium heat for 1-2 minutes on each side, or wrap in foil and warm in the oven.
4. **Stuff Pita:**
    - Gently open each pita pocket and fill with the chickpea and spinach mixture.
5. **Serve:**
    - Optionally, serve with a dollop of plain Greek yogurt or tzatziki and lemon wedges on the side.

Enjoy your nutritious and satisfying Chickpea and Spinach Stuffed Pita!

Almond Flour Muffins with Blueberries
Ingredients:

2 cups almond flour
1/2 cup coconut flour (or additional almond flour if you prefer)
1/2 teaspoon baking soda
1/4 teaspoon salt
1/4 cup honey or maple syrup
1/4 cup coconut oil or butter, melted
3 large eggs
1 teaspoon vanilla extract
1 cup fresh or frozen blueberries (if using frozen, do not thaw)
Instructions:

Preheat Oven: Preheat your oven to 350°F (175°C). Line a muffin tin with paper liners or lightly grease it.

Mix Dry Ingredients: In a large bowl, combine almond flour, coconut flour, baking soda, and salt. Mix well.

Mix Wet Ingredients: In another bowl, whisk together honey or maple syrup, melted coconut oil or butter, eggs, and vanilla extract until well combined.

Combine Ingredients: Pour the wet ingredients into the dry ingredients and mix until just combined. Gently fold in the blueberries.

Fill Muffin Tin: Divide the batter evenly among the muffin cups, filling each about 3/4 full.

Bake: Bake in the preheated oven for 20-25 minutes, or until a toothpick inserted into the center comes out clean and the tops are golden brown.

Cool: Allow the muffins to cool in the pan for about 10 minutes before transferring to a wire rack to cool completely.

Enjoy your moist and flavorful almond flour muffins with blueberries!

Veggie-Packed Quiche with a Sweet Potato Crust

Ingredients:

- **For the Sweet Potato Crust:**
    - 2 medium sweet potatoes, peeled and grated
    - 1 tablespoon olive oil
    - 1/2 teaspoon salt
    - 1/4 teaspoon black pepper
    - 1/4 teaspoon paprika (optional)
- **For the Quiche Filling:**
    - 1 tablespoon olive oil
    - 1 small onion, diced
    - 1 red bell pepper, diced
    - 1 cup fresh spinach, chopped
    - 1 cup mushrooms, sliced
    - 4 large eggs
    - 1/2 cup milk (dairy or non-dairy)
    - 1 cup shredded cheese (e.g., cheddar, feta, or mozzarella)
    - Salt and pepper, to taste
    - 1/2 teaspoon dried thyme or oregano (optional)

Instructions:

1. **Preheat Oven:** Preheat your oven to 375°F (190°C).
2. **Prepare Sweet Potato Crust:**
    - Heat olive oil in a skillet over medium heat. Add grated sweet potatoes, salt, pepper, and paprika. Cook for about 5 minutes until they start to soften.
    - Press the cooked sweet potatoes into the bottom and up the sides of a lightly greased pie dish or quiche pan to form an even crust. Bake in the preheated oven for 15 minutes.
3. **Prepare the Quiche Filling:**
    - While the crust is baking, heat olive oil in a skillet over medium heat. Add onion, bell pepper, mushrooms, and cook until softened, about 5-7 minutes. Stir in chopped spinach and cook until wilted. Season with salt and pepper.
    - In a bowl, whisk together eggs, milk, and dried thyme or oregano. Stir in shredded cheese.
4. **Assemble Quiche:**
    - Remove the sweet potato crust from the oven. Spread the veggie mixture evenly over the crust.
    - Pour the egg and cheese mixture over the veggies.
5. **Bake:** Return the quiche to the oven and bake for 25-30 minutes, or until the quiche is set and lightly golden on top.

6. **Cool and Serve:** Allow the quiche to cool slightly before slicing. Serve warm or at room temperature.

Enjoy your delicious and healthy veggie-packed quiche with a sweet potato crust!

Peanut Butter and Strawberry Chia Jam Sandwich

Ingredients:

- **For the Strawberry Chia Jam:**
    - 1 cup fresh or frozen strawberries
    - 2 tablespoons chia seeds
    - 1-2 tablespoons honey or maple syrup (adjust to taste)
    - 1 teaspoon lemon juice (optional, for a tangy flavor)
- **For the Sandwich:**
    - 2 slices whole grain or your preferred bread
    - 2 tablespoons peanut butter

Instructions:

1. **Make the Strawberry Chia Jam:**
    - In a saucepan, heat the strawberries over medium heat, mashing them with a fork or potato masher until they start to break down.
    - Stir in chia seeds and honey or maple syrup. Cook for 5-7 minutes, stirring frequently, until the mixture thickens to a jam-like consistency.
    - Remove from heat and stir in lemon juice if using. Allow to cool completely.
2. **Assemble the Sandwich:**
    - Spread peanut butter evenly over one slice of bread.
    - Spread the cooled strawberry chia jam over the other slice of bread.
    - Press the two slices together to form a sandwich.

Enjoy your delicious and nutritious Peanut Butter and Strawberry Chia Jam Sandwich!

Egg and Avocado Breakfast Quesadilla

Ingredients:

- 2 large flour tortillas
- 2 large eggs
- 1 ripe avocado, sliced
- 1/2 cup shredded cheese (e.g., cheddar, Monterey Jack, or your favorite)
- 1 tablespoon olive oil or butter
- Salt and pepper, to taste
- Optional: diced tomatoes, chopped cilantro, or hot sauce for extra flavor

Instructions:

1. **Cook the Eggs:**
    - Heat a non-stick skillet over medium heat and add olive oil or butter.
    - Crack the eggs into the skillet and scramble them, cooking until fully set. Season with salt and pepper. Remove from heat.
2. **Assemble the Quesadilla:**
    - Place one tortilla in the skillet over medium heat. Sprinkle half of the shredded cheese evenly over the tortilla.
    - Spread the scrambled eggs over the cheese, and then layer with avocado slices. Add additional toppings like diced tomatoes or cilantro if desired.
    - Sprinkle the remaining cheese on top and cover with the second tortilla.
3. **Cook the Quesadilla:**
    - Cook for 2-3 minutes on each side, or until the tortilla is golden brown and the cheese is melted. Use a spatula to flip it carefully.
4. **Serve:**
    - Remove from heat and let it cool slightly before cutting into wedges. Serve with hot sauce if desired.

Enjoy your flavorful and satisfying Egg and Avocado Breakfast Quesadilla!

Mediterranean Breakfast Bowl with Quinoa

Ingredients:

- **For the Quinoa:**
  - 1 cup quinoa, rinsed
  - 2 cups water or vegetable broth
- **For the Bowl:**
  - 1 cup cherry tomatoes, halved
  - 1/2 cucumber, diced
  - 1/4 cup Kalamata olives, sliced
  - 1/4 cup crumbled feta cheese
  - 1/4 red onion, thinly sliced
  - 1/4 cup fresh parsley or basil, chopped
  - 1 avocado, sliced
- **For the Dressing:**
  - 3 tablespoons extra-virgin olive oil
  - 1 tablespoon red wine vinegar
  - 1 teaspoon lemon juice
  - 1 teaspoon Dijon mustard
  - 1 clove garlic, minced
  - Salt and pepper, to taste

Instructions:

1. **Cook the Quinoa:**
   - In a medium saucepan, bring the water or vegetable broth to a boil.
   - Add the rinsed quinoa, reduce heat to low, cover, and simmer for about 15 minutes, or until the quinoa is cooked and the liquid is absorbed. Fluff with a fork and let it cool slightly.
2. **Prepare the Vegetables:**
   - While the quinoa is cooking, prepare the cherry tomatoes, cucumber, olives, feta cheese, red onion, parsley or basil, and avocado.
3. **Make the Dressing:**
   - In a small bowl, whisk together olive oil, red wine vinegar, lemon juice, Dijon mustard, minced garlic, salt, and pepper.
4. **Assemble the Breakfast Bowl:**
   - In serving bowls, add a portion of cooked quinoa.
   - Arrange the cherry tomatoes, cucumber, olives, feta cheese, red onion, and avocado on top of the quinoa.
   - Drizzle with the prepared dressing.
5. **Garnish and Serve:**
   - Garnish with additional fresh herbs if desired.
   - Serve immediately or refrigerate for later.

Enjoy your Mediterranean Breakfast Bowl with Quinoa—perfect for a nutritious and satisfying start to your day!

Cucumber and Hummus Sandwiches

Ingredients:

- 8 slices of whole grain or your preferred bread
- 1 cup hummus (store-bought or homemade)
- 1 cucumber, thinly sliced
- 1/4 cup fresh dill or mint, chopped (optional)
- Salt and pepper, to taste
- 1 tablespoon olive oil (optional, for drizzling)
- Lemon zest (optional, for added flavor)

Instructions:

1. **Prepare the Ingredients:**
   - Wash and thinly slice the cucumber. You can slice them into rounds or thin strips, depending on your preference.
   - If using, chop fresh dill or mint for garnish.
2. **Assemble the Sandwiches:**
   - Spread a generous layer of hummus on one side of each slice of bread.
   - Arrange the cucumber slices evenly over the hummus on four of the bread slices.
   - Sprinkle with salt, pepper, and chopped dill or mint if using.
   - Optionally, drizzle with a little olive oil and sprinkle with lemon zest for extra flavor.
3. **Finish the Sandwiches:**
   - Top with the remaining bread slices, hummus side down, to form sandwiches.
   - Slice the sandwiches into halves or quarters, if desired.
4. **Serve:**
   - Serve immediately, or wrap them up for a quick lunch or snack.

These Cucumber and Hummus Sandwiches are light, flavorful, and perfect for a quick and healthy meal!

Spicy Black Bean and Sweet Potato Tacos

Ingredients:

- **For the Tacos:**
    - 1 large sweet potato, peeled and diced
    - 1 tablespoon olive oil
    - 1 teaspoon ground cumin
    - 1 teaspoon smoked paprika
    - 1/2 teaspoon chili powder
    - 1/4 teaspoon cayenne pepper (optional, for extra heat)
    - 1 can (15 oz) black beans, drained and rinsed
    - 1 cup corn kernels (fresh, frozen, or canned)
    - 1/4 cup fresh cilantro, chopped
    - 8 small tortillas (corn or flour)
- **For the Toppings:**
    - 1 avocado, sliced or diced
    - 1/2 red onion, thinly sliced
    - 1 cup shredded lettuce or cabbage
    - 1/2 cup crumbled feta cheese or shredded cheese (optional)
    - Lime wedges
    - Salsa or hot sauce (optional)

Instructions:

1. **Prepare the Sweet Potatoes:**
    - Preheat your oven to 400°F (200°C).
    - Toss the diced sweet potato with olive oil, ground cumin, smoked paprika, chili powder, and cayenne pepper (if using). Spread on a baking sheet in a single layer.
    - Roast in the preheated oven for 20-25 minutes, or until tender and lightly caramelized, stirring halfway through.
2. **Cook the Black Beans and Corn:**
    - While the sweet potatoes are roasting, heat a small skillet over medium heat. Add a splash of olive oil if desired.
    - Add the black beans and corn. Cook, stirring occasionally, until heated through and slightly golden, about 5-7 minutes.
    - Stir in fresh cilantro and season with salt and pepper to taste.
3. **Warm the Tortillas:**
    - Warm the tortillas in a dry skillet over medium heat for 30 seconds to 1 minute on each side, or until pliable. You can also warm them in the oven wrapped in foil.
4. **Assemble the Tacos:**

- Fill each tortilla with a portion of roasted sweet potatoes and the black bean-corn mixture.
- Top with avocado slices, red onion, shredded lettuce or cabbage, and crumbled feta cheese or shredded cheese if using.

5. **Serve:**
    - Serve the tacos with lime wedges for squeezing over the top and salsa or hot sauce if desired.

Enjoy your delicious and spicy Black Bean and Sweet Potato Tacos!

Carrot and Zucchini Fritters

Ingredients:

- 1 medium carrot, grated
- 1 medium zucchini, grated
- 1/2 small onion, finely diced
- 2 cloves garlic, minced
- 1/4 cup all-purpose flour (or gluten-free flour)
- 1/4 cup grated Parmesan cheese (optional)
- 2 large eggs
- 1 teaspoon dried oregano or thyme
- Salt and pepper, to taste
- 2 tablespoons olive oil or vegetable oil (for frying)

Instructions:

1. **Prepare Vegetables:**
   - Place the grated carrot and zucchini in a clean kitchen towel or cheesecloth. Squeeze out as much excess moisture as possible.
2. **Mix Ingredients:**
   - In a large bowl, combine the grated carrot, zucchini, diced onion, minced garlic, flour, Parmesan cheese (if using), eggs, dried oregano or thyme, salt, and pepper. Mix until well combined.
3. **Heat the Oil:**
   - Heat olive oil or vegetable oil in a large skillet over medium heat.
4. **Form and Cook Fritters:**
   - Scoop spoonfuls of the mixture into the skillet, flattening them slightly with the back of the spoon to form fritters.
   - Cook for 3-4 minutes on each side, or until golden brown and crispy.
5. **Drain and Serve:**
   - Remove the fritters from the skillet and drain on paper towels.
   - Serve warm with a dollop of Greek yogurt or a side of salsa if desired.

Enjoy your crispy and flavorful Carrot and Zucchini Fritters!

Smoked Salmon and Avocado Salad

Ingredients:

- 4 oz smoked salmon, sliced or torn into pieces
- 1 ripe avocado, diced
- 4 cups mixed greens or baby spinach
- 1/2 small red onion, thinly sliced
- 1/2 cucumber, sliced
- 1/4 cup capers, drained (optional)
- 1 tablespoon fresh dill or chives, chopped (optional)
- **For the Dressing:**
    - 2 tablespoons extra-virgin olive oil
    - 1 tablespoon lemon juice
    - 1 teaspoon Dijon mustard
    - 1 teaspoon honey or maple syrup
    - Salt and pepper, to taste

Instructions:

1. **Prepare the Salad:**
    - In a large salad bowl, combine mixed greens, diced avocado, sliced red onion, cucumber, and capers if using.
2. **Make the Dressing:**
    - In a small bowl or jar, whisk together olive oil, lemon juice, Dijon mustard, honey or maple syrup, salt, and pepper until well combined.
3. **Assemble the Salad:**
    - Gently toss the salad ingredients with the dressing.
    - Top with pieces of smoked salmon and sprinkle with fresh dill or chives if desired.
4. **Serve:**
    - Serve immediately or chill briefly before serving.

Enjoy your light and flavorful Smoked Salmon and Avocado Salad!

Edamame and Corn Salad

Ingredients:

- 1 cup frozen edamame, thawed and shelled
- 1 cup corn kernels (fresh, frozen, or canned, drained)
- 1 red bell pepper, diced
- 1/4 cup red onion, finely chopped
- 1/4 cup fresh cilantro or parsley, chopped
- 1 avocado, diced (optional)
- **For the Dressing:**
    - 3 tablespoons extra-virgin olive oil
    - 2 tablespoons lime juice
    - 1 teaspoon honey or maple syrup
    - 1 clove garlic, minced
    - Salt and pepper, to taste

Instructions:

1. **Prepare the Vegetables:**
    - In a large bowl, combine the edamame, corn, diced red bell pepper, and chopped red onion.
2. **Make the Dressing:**
    - In a small bowl or jar, whisk together olive oil, lime juice, honey or maple syrup, minced garlic, salt, and pepper until well combined.
3. **Assemble the Salad:**
    - Pour the dressing over the vegetable mixture and toss to coat evenly.
    - Gently fold in diced avocado if using.
4. **Serve:**
    - Garnish with fresh cilantro or parsley and serve immediately or chill in the refrigerator before serving.

Enjoy your refreshing and nutritious Edamame and Corn Salad!

Protein-Packed Breakfast Smoothie with Spinach

Ingredients:

- 1 cup fresh spinach leaves
- 1/2 cup Greek yogurt (plain or vanilla)
- 1/2 cup milk (dairy or non-dairy, e.g., almond, soy, oat)
- 1 banana, peeled and sliced
- 1/2 cup frozen berries (e.g., blueberries, strawberries, or mixed)
- 1 scoop protein powder (vanilla or unflavored)
- 1 tablespoon chia seeds or flaxseeds (optional, for added fiber)
- 1 tablespoon honey or maple syrup (optional, for sweetness)
- Ice cubes (optional, for a thicker smoothie)

Instructions:

1. **Blend the Ingredients:**
   - In a blender, combine the spinach, Greek yogurt, milk, banana, frozen berries, and protein powder.
   - If using chia seeds or flaxseeds, add them to the blender.
   - Blend on high until smooth and creamy. Add honey or maple syrup if desired for extra sweetness.
   - If you prefer a thicker smoothie, add a few ice cubes and blend again.
2. **Serve:**
   - Pour the smoothie into a glass or travel cup.
3. **Optional Garnishes:**
   - Garnish with a few fresh berries or a sprinkle of chia seeds on top.

Enjoy your refreshing and protein-packed breakfast smoothie with spinach!

Whole Grain French Toast with Fresh Berries

Ingredients:

- **For the French Toast:**
    - 4 slices whole grain bread
    - 2 large eggs
    - 1/2 cup milk (dairy or non-dairy)
    - 1/2 teaspoon vanilla extract
    - 1/2 teaspoon ground cinnamon
    - A pinch of salt
    - 1 tablespoon butter or oil (for cooking)
- **For the Topping:**
    - 1 cup fresh berries (e.g., strawberries, blueberries, raspberries)
    - 2 tablespoons maple syrup or honey (for drizzling)
    - Optional: powdered sugar for dusting

Instructions:

1. **Prepare the Batter:**
    - In a shallow bowl or dish, whisk together eggs, milk, vanilla extract, ground cinnamon, and a pinch of salt.
2. **Heat the Pan:**
    - Heat a skillet or griddle over medium heat and add a tablespoon of butter or oil. Allow it to melt and coat the surface.
3. **Dip and Cook the Bread:**
    - Dip each slice of whole grain bread into the egg mixture, ensuring both sides are coated. Let any excess drip off.
    - Place the bread slices on the heated skillet and cook for 2-3 minutes on each side, or until golden brown and cooked through.
4. **Prepare the Berries:**
    - While the French toast is cooking, rinse the fresh berries and pat them dry.
5. **Assemble the French Toast:**
    - Serve the French toast warm, topped with fresh berries.
    - Drizzle with maple syrup or honey.
    - Optionally, dust with powdered sugar for an extra touch of sweetness.

Enjoy your wholesome and delicious Whole Grain French Toast with Fresh Berries!

Apple and Walnut Oat Muffins

Ingredients:

- **For the Muffins:**
    - 1 cup rolled oats
    - 1 cup whole wheat flour or all-purpose flour
    - 1/2 cup brown sugar or coconut sugar
    - 1 teaspoon baking powder
    - 1/2 teaspoon baking soda
    - 1/2 teaspoon ground cinnamon
    - 1/4 teaspoon ground nutmeg (optional)
    - 1/4 teaspoon salt
    - 1/2 cup chopped walnuts
    - 1 cup apple, peeled and diced (about 1 medium apple)
    - 1/2 cup unsweetened applesauce
    - 1/4 cup vegetable oil or melted coconut oil
    - 2 large eggs
    - 1 teaspoon vanilla extract
- **For the Topping (optional):**
    - 2 tablespoons rolled oats
    - 1 tablespoon brown sugar
    - 1 tablespoon chopped walnuts

Instructions:

1. **Preheat Oven:**
    - Preheat your oven to 375°F (190°C). Line a muffin tin with paper liners or lightly grease it.
2. **Prepare Dry Ingredients:**
    - In a large bowl, combine rolled oats, flour, brown sugar, baking powder, baking soda, cinnamon, nutmeg (if using), salt, and chopped walnuts.
3. **Mix Wet Ingredients:**
    - In another bowl, whisk together applesauce, oil, eggs, and vanilla extract until well combined.
4. **Combine Ingredients:**
    - Add the wet ingredients to the dry ingredients and mix until just combined.
    - Gently fold in the diced apple.
5. **Fill Muffin Tin:**
    - Divide the batter evenly among the muffin cups, filling each about 3/4 full.
6. **Prepare Topping (optional):**
    - If using the topping, mix rolled oats, brown sugar, and chopped walnuts together. Sprinkle this mixture evenly over the muffin batter.
7. **Bake:**

- Bake in the preheated oven for 18-22 minutes, or until a toothpick inserted into the center of a muffin comes out clean.
8. **Cool:**
    - Allow the muffins to cool in the pan for about 10 minutes before transferring them to a wire rack to cool completely.

Enjoy your wholesome and delicious Apple and Walnut Oat Muffins!

Sweet Potato and Black Bean Enchiladas

Ingredients:

- **For the Enchiladas:**
    - 2 medium sweet potatoes, peeled and diced
    - 1 can (15 oz) black beans, drained and rinsed
    - 1 cup corn kernels (fresh, frozen, or canned, drained)
    - 1 red bell pepper, diced
    - 1 small onion, diced
    - 2 cloves garlic, minced
    - 1 teaspoon ground cumin
    - 1 teaspoon smoked paprika
    - 1/2 teaspoon chili powder
    - Salt and pepper, to taste
    - 8-10 corn or flour tortillas
- **For the Enchilada Sauce:**
    - 1 can (15 oz) tomato sauce
    - 1/4 cup tomato paste
    - 1 cup vegetable or chicken broth
    - 1 tablespoon chili powder
    - 1 teaspoon ground cumin
    - 1/2 teaspoon smoked paprika
    - 1/4 teaspoon garlic powder
    - 1/4 teaspoon onion powder
    - Salt and pepper, to taste
- **For the Topping:**
    - 1 cup shredded cheese (e.g., cheddar, Monterey Jack, or a dairy-free alternative)
    - Fresh cilantro, chopped (for garnish)
    - Sliced avocado or guacamole (optional)
    - Sour cream or Greek yogurt (optional)

Instructions:

1. **Prepare the Sweet Potatoes:**
    - Preheat your oven to 400°F (200°C).
    - Toss the diced sweet potatoes with a little olive oil, salt, and pepper. Spread them out on a baking sheet in a single layer.
    - Roast in the preheated oven for 20-25 minutes, or until tender and slightly caramelized. Remove from the oven and set aside.
2. **Prepare the Enchilada Sauce:**
    - In a medium saucepan, combine tomato sauce, tomato paste, vegetable or chicken broth, chili powder, ground cumin, smoked paprika, garlic powder, onion powder, salt, and pepper.

- Simmer over medium heat for about 10 minutes, stirring occasionally, until slightly thickened. Adjust seasoning to taste.

3. **Prepare the Filling:**
    - In a large skillet, heat a little olive oil over medium heat. Add the diced onion and bell pepper, and cook until softened, about 5 minutes.
    - Add the minced garlic, cumin, smoked paprika, and chili powder. Cook for another 1-2 minutes.
    - Stir in the black beans, corn, and roasted sweet potatoes. Cook for another 2-3 minutes, then remove from heat.

4. **Assemble the Enchiladas:**
    - Spread a small amount of the enchilada sauce in the bottom of a baking dish.
    - Warm the tortillas slightly if they are stiff, so they are easier to roll.
    - Spoon some of the sweet potato and black bean mixture onto each tortilla, then roll them up and place seam-side down in the baking dish.
    - Pour the remaining enchilada sauce over the top of the rolled tortillas, and sprinkle with shredded cheese.

5. **Bake:**
    - Cover the baking dish with foil and bake in the preheated oven for 20 minutes. Remove the foil and bake for an additional 10 minutes, or until the cheese is melted and bubbly.

6. **Serve:**
    - Garnish with fresh cilantro, and serve with sliced avocado or guacamole, and sour cream or Greek yogurt if desired.

Enjoy your delicious and satisfying Sweet Potato and Black Bean Enchiladas!

Baked Eggplant with Tomato and Basil

Ingredients:

- 1 large eggplant, sliced into 1/2-inch rounds
- 1 cup cherry tomatoes, halved (or 2 medium tomatoes, diced)
- 2 tablespoons olive oil
- 2 cloves garlic, minced
- 1 teaspoon dried oregano
- 1/2 teaspoon dried basil (or 1 tablespoon fresh basil, chopped)
- Salt and pepper, to taste
- 1/4 cup grated Parmesan cheese (optional)
- Fresh basil leaves, for garnish

Instructions:

1. **Preheat Oven:**
   - Preheat your oven to 400°F (200°C). Line a baking sheet with parchment paper or lightly grease it.
2. **Prepare the Eggplant:**
   - Arrange the eggplant slices on the baking sheet in a single layer. Brush both sides of each slice with olive oil and season with salt and pepper.
   - Bake in the preheated oven for about 20 minutes, flipping halfway through, until the eggplant is tender and slightly golden.
3. **Prepare the Tomato Mixture:**
   - While the eggplant is baking, heat a tablespoon of olive oil in a skillet over medium heat. Add the minced garlic and cook for about 1 minute until fragrant.
   - Add the cherry tomatoes (or diced tomatoes) to the skillet. Stir in dried oregano, dried basil (or fresh basil), salt, and pepper. Cook for 5-7 minutes, until the tomatoes are softened and slightly saucy. Adjust seasoning as needed.
4. **Assemble the Dish:**
   - Once the eggplant is done baking, remove it from the oven and spoon the tomato mixture evenly over each slice of eggplant.
   - If using Parmesan cheese, sprinkle it on top of the tomato mixture.
5. **Bake Again:**
   - Return the baking sheet to the oven and bake for an additional 5-10 minutes, or until the cheese is melted and bubbly, and the tomatoes are slightly caramelized.
6. **Garnish and Serve:**
   - Remove from the oven and garnish with fresh basil leaves.
   - Serve warm as a side dish or a light main course.

Enjoy your delicious Baked Eggplant with Tomato and Basil!

Fresh Fruit Salad with Mint

Ingredients:

- 2 cups strawberries, hulled and sliced
- 2 cups blueberries
- 2 cups watermelon, cubed
- 1 cup kiwi, peeled and sliced
- 1 cup pineapple, cubed
- 1 tablespoon honey or maple syrup (optional, for added sweetness)
- 1 tablespoon fresh mint leaves, chopped
- 1 tablespoon lime juice (optional, for extra zing)

Instructions:

1. **Prepare the Fruit:**
   - In a large bowl, combine strawberries, blueberries, watermelon, kiwi, and pineapple.
2. **Add Sweetener (Optional):**
   - If desired, drizzle with honey or maple syrup and gently toss to combine.
3. **Add Mint and Lime Juice:**
   - Sprinkle chopped mint leaves over the fruit salad.
   - If using, drizzle with lime juice and toss gently to mix.
4. **Serve:**
   - Chill in the refrigerator for about 30 minutes before serving to let the flavors meld.

Enjoy your vibrant and refreshing Fresh Fruit Salad with Mint!

Smashed Chickpea and Avocado Toast

Ingredients:

- 1 can (15 oz) chickpeas, drained and rinsed
- 1 ripe avocado
- 1 tablespoon lemon juice
- 1 tablespoon olive oil
- 1 clove garlic, minced
- Salt and pepper, to taste
- 1/4 teaspoon ground cumin (optional)
- 1/4 teaspoon red pepper flakes (optional, for heat)
- 4 slices whole grain or your preferred bread
- Fresh parsley or cilantro, chopped (for garnish)
- Cherry tomatoes, sliced (for topping, optional)

Instructions:

1. **Prepare the Chickpeas:**
    - In a bowl, use a fork or a potato masher to lightly mash the chickpeas. You want to leave some chunks for texture.
2. **Prepare the Avocado Mixture:**
    - In another bowl, mash the avocado with lemon juice, olive oil, minced garlic, salt, pepper, ground cumin (if using), and red pepper flakes (if using) until smooth but still slightly chunky.
3. **Combine Chickpeas and Avocado:**
    - Gently fold the mashed chickpeas into the avocado mixture until well combined.
4. **Toast the Bread:**
    - Toast the slices of bread to your desired level of crispiness.
5. **Assemble the Toast:**
    - Spread a generous layer of the smashed chickpea and avocado mixture onto each slice of toasted bread.
6. **Garnish and Serve:**
    - Garnish with chopped parsley or cilantro.
    - Add sliced cherry tomatoes on top if desired.

Enjoy your nutritious and flavorful Smashed Chickpea and Avocado Toast!

Low-Carb Greek Chicken Skewers

Ingredients:

- **For the Chicken Marinade:**
    - 1 pound boneless, skinless chicken breasts or thighs, cut into bite-sized pieces
    - 1/4 cup extra-virgin olive oil
    - 3 tablespoons lemon juice (about 1 lemon)
    - 3 cloves garlic, minced
    - 1 tablespoon dried oregano
    - 1 teaspoon ground cumin
    - 1/2 teaspoon paprika
    - 1/2 teaspoon salt
    - 1/4 teaspoon black pepper
- **For the Tzatziki Sauce (optional):**
    - 1 cup Greek yogurt (plain, unsweetened)
    - 1/2 cucumber, grated and excess moisture squeezed out
    - 1 clove garlic, minced
    - 1 tablespoon lemon juice
    - 1 tablespoon fresh dill, chopped (or 1 teaspoon dried dill)
    - Salt and pepper, to taste
- **For the Skewers:**
    - 1 red bell pepper, cut into chunks
    - 1 green bell pepper, cut into chunks
    - 1 small red onion, cut into chunks
    - 1 cup cherry tomatoes

Instructions:

1. **Marinate the Chicken:**
    - In a large bowl, combine olive oil, lemon juice, minced garlic, dried oregano, ground cumin, paprika, salt, and black pepper.
    - Add the chicken pieces to the marinade and toss to coat evenly. Cover and refrigerate for at least 30 minutes, or up to 2 hours for more flavor.
2. **Prepare the Tzatziki Sauce (if using):**
    - In a bowl, mix together Greek yogurt, grated cucumber, minced garlic, lemon juice, and dill.
    - Season with salt and pepper to taste. Cover and refrigerate until ready to use.
3. **Assemble the Skewers:**
    - Preheat your grill or grill pan to medium-high heat.
    - Thread the marinated chicken pieces onto skewers, alternating with chunks of bell pepper, red onion, and cherry tomatoes.
4. **Grill the Skewers:**

- Place the skewers on the grill and cook for 10-12 minutes, turning occasionally, until the chicken is fully cooked and has an internal temperature of 165°F (74°C).
5. **Serve:**
    - Serve the chicken skewers with a side of Tzatziki sauce for dipping, if desired.
    - Garnish with additional fresh dill or lemon wedges, if preferred.

Enjoy your delicious and low-carb Greek Chicken Skewers!

Tofu and Veggie Stir-Fry

Ingredients:

- **For the Stir-Fry:**
    - 1 block (14 oz) firm tofu, drained and pressed
    - 2 tablespoons vegetable oil or sesame oil (for frying)
    - 1 red bell pepper, sliced
    - 1 green bell pepper, sliced
    - 1 medium carrot, sliced into thin rounds or julienned
    - 1 cup broccoli florets
    - 1 cup snap peas or snow peas
    - 1 small onion, sliced
    - 2 cloves garlic, minced
    - 1 tablespoon fresh ginger, minced
    - 2 green onions, sliced (optional, for garnish)
- **For the Sauce:**
    - 1/4 cup soy sauce or tamari (for gluten-free)
    - 2 tablespoons hoisin sauce
    - 1 tablespoon rice vinegar
    - 1 tablespoon sesame oil
    - 1 tablespoon cornstarch mixed with 2 tablespoons water (for thickening)
    - 1 teaspoon brown sugar or honey (optional, for sweetness)
    - 1/2 teaspoon red pepper flakes (optional, for heat)

Instructions:

1. **Prepare the Tofu:**
    - Cut the pressed tofu into bite-sized cubes.
    - Heat 2 tablespoons of vegetable oil or sesame oil in a large skillet or wok over medium-high heat.
    - Add the tofu cubes and cook until golden brown and crispy on all sides, about 8-10 minutes. Remove the tofu from the skillet and set aside.
2. **Prepare the Vegetables:**
    - In the same skillet or wok, add a little more oil if needed.
    - Add the sliced onion, bell peppers, carrot, broccoli, and snap peas. Stir-fry for 5-7 minutes, or until the vegetables are tender-crisp.
    - Add minced garlic and ginger, and stir-fry for another 1-2 minutes until fragrant.
3. **Make the Sauce:**
    - In a small bowl, whisk together soy sauce, hoisin sauce, rice vinegar, sesame oil, and brown sugar (if using).
    - Stir in the cornstarch-water mixture to thicken the sauce.
4. **Combine and Cook:**
    - Return the cooked tofu to the skillet with the vegetables.

- Pour the sauce over the tofu and vegetables, stirring to coat evenly.
- Cook for an additional 2-3 minutes, or until the sauce has thickened and everything is heated through.

5. **Serve:**
    - Garnish with sliced green onions if desired.
    - Serve the stir-fry over cooked rice, quinoa, or noodles.

Enjoy your vibrant and delicious Tofu and Veggie Stir-Fry!

Pumpkin Spice Overnight Oats

Ingredients:

- 1/2 cup rolled oats
- 1/2 cup milk (dairy or non-dairy, e.g., almond, oat)
- 1/2 cup canned pumpkin puree (not pumpkin pie filling)
- 1/4 cup Greek yogurt (plain or vanilla)
- 1 tablespoon maple syrup or honey
- 1/2 teaspoon pumpkin pie spice (or a mix of cinnamon, nutmeg, and ginger)
- 1/4 teaspoon vanilla extract
- A pinch of salt
- **Optional Toppings:**
    - Chopped nuts (e.g., pecans or walnuts)
    - Dried cranberries or raisins
    - A sprinkle of additional pumpkin pie spice
    - Fresh fruit or apple slices

Instructions:

1. **Combine Ingredients:**
    - In a jar or airtight container, mix together the rolled oats, milk, pumpkin puree, Greek yogurt, maple syrup or honey, pumpkin pie spice, vanilla extract, and a pinch of salt.
2. **Stir and Refrigerate:**
    - Stir the mixture well to combine. Ensure the oats are fully submerged in the liquid.
    - Cover and refrigerate overnight, or for at least 4 hours.
3. **Serve:**
    - In the morning, give the oats a good stir. Adjust sweetness or add a splash of milk if needed.
    - Top with your choice of optional toppings such as chopped nuts, dried cranberries, or fresh fruit.

Enjoy your warm and comforting Pumpkin Spice Overnight Oats!

Pita Bread with Spinach and Feta

Ingredients:

- 4 whole wheat or regular pita bread
- 1 cup fresh spinach, chopped (or 1/2 cup frozen spinach, thawed and squeezed dry)
- 1/2 cup crumbled feta cheese
- 1/2 cup shredded mozzarella or cheddar cheese (optional, for extra gooeyness)
- 1 tablespoon olive oil
- 1 clove garlic, minced
- 1/4 teaspoon dried oregano or basil
- Salt and pepper, to taste
- Optional: cherry tomatoes, halved, or sliced olives for extra flavor

Instructions:

1. **Preheat Oven:**
    - Preheat your oven to 375°F (190°C).
2. **Prepare the Spinach Mixture:**
    - In a skillet over medium heat, add the olive oil and minced garlic. Sauté for about 1 minute, or until the garlic is fragrant.
    - Add the chopped spinach and cook for 2-3 minutes, until wilted and any excess moisture is evaporated.
    - Season with salt, pepper, and dried oregano or basil. Remove from heat and let cool slightly.
3. **Assemble the Pita Bread:**
    - Place the pita bread on a baking sheet.
    - Spread an even layer of the spinach mixture over each pita.
    - Sprinkle crumbled feta cheese evenly over the spinach. Add shredded mozzarella or cheddar cheese if using.
    - Optionally, top with cherry tomato halves or sliced olives.
4. **Bake:**
    - Bake in the preheated oven for 10-12 minutes, or until the pita is crispy and the cheese is melted and slightly golden.
5. **Serve:**
    - Remove from the oven and let cool slightly before slicing into wedges.
    - Serve warm as a snack, appetizer, or light meal.

Enjoy your flavorful Pita Bread with Spinach and Feta!

Almond-Crusted Baked Chicken Tenders

Ingredients:

- **For the Chicken Tenders:**
    - 1 pound chicken tenders (or chicken breasts cut into strips)
    - 1 cup almond flour or finely chopped almonds
    - 1/2 cup grated Parmesan cheese (optional for extra flavor)
    - 1 teaspoon paprika
    - 1/2 teaspoon garlic powder
    - 1/2 teaspoon onion powder
    - 1/2 teaspoon dried oregano or dried thyme
    - Salt and pepper, to taste
    - 2 large eggs
    - 2 tablespoons water or milk (optional, to thin out the egg wash)
- **For Serving (optional):**
    - Fresh lemon wedges
    - Your favorite dipping sauce (e.g., honey mustard, ranch, or barbecue sauce)

Instructions:

1. **Preheat Oven:**
    - Preheat your oven to 400°F (200°C). Line a baking sheet with parchment paper or lightly grease it.
2. **Prepare the Breading:**
    - In a shallow dish or bowl, combine almond flour, grated Parmesan cheese (if using), paprika, garlic powder, onion powder, dried oregano, salt, and pepper.
3. **Prepare the Egg Wash:**
    - In another shallow dish, beat the eggs with a tablespoon of water or milk (if using).
4. **Bread the Chicken:**
    - Dip each chicken tender into the egg wash, allowing any excess to drip off.
    - Coat the chicken tender with the almond flour mixture, pressing gently to adhere.
5. **Bake the Chicken:**
    - Arrange the breaded chicken tenders on the prepared baking sheet in a single layer.
    - Bake in the preheated oven for 15-20 minutes, or until the chicken is cooked through and the coating is golden brown and crispy. The internal temperature of the chicken should reach 165°F (74°C).
6. **Serve:**
    - Remove the chicken tenders from the oven and let them cool slightly.
    - Serve with fresh lemon wedges and your favorite dipping sauce, if desired.

Enjoy your crispy and delicious Almond-Crusted Baked Chicken Tenders!

Butternut Squash and Kale Salad

Ingredients:

- **For the Salad:**
    - 1 small butternut squash, peeled, seeded, and cubed
    - 1 tablespoon olive oil
    - Salt and pepper, to taste
    - 4 cups kale, stems removed and leaves chopped
    - 1/4 cup dried cranberries or pomegranate seeds
    - 1/4 cup crumbled feta cheese or goat cheese
    - 1/4 cup toasted pecans or walnuts (optional)
    - 1 apple or pear, cored and thinly sliced (optional)
- **For the Dressing:**
    - 3 tablespoons olive oil
    - 2 tablespoons apple cider vinegar or balsamic vinegar
    - 1 tablespoon maple syrup or honey
    - 1 teaspoon Dijon mustard
    - Salt and pepper, to taste

Instructions:

1. **Roast the Butternut Squash:**
    - Preheat your oven to 400°F (200°C). Line a baking sheet with parchment paper.
    - Toss the butternut squash cubes with olive oil, salt, and pepper. Spread them out on the baking sheet.
    - Roast for 20-25 minutes, or until tender and slightly caramelized, stirring halfway through. Allow to cool slightly.
2. **Prepare the Kale:**
    - While the squash is roasting, massage the chopped kale with a bit of olive oil and a pinch of salt until the leaves are softened and darkened. This helps to reduce the bitterness of the kale.
3. **Make the Dressing:**
    - In a small bowl or jar, whisk together olive oil, apple cider vinegar, maple syrup, Dijon mustard, salt, and pepper until well combined.
4. **Assemble the Salad:**
    - In a large bowl, combine the massaged kale, roasted butternut squash, dried cranberries, crumbled feta, and toasted nuts if using.
    - Drizzle with the dressing and toss gently to coat.
5. **Serve:**
    - Top with thinly sliced apple or pear if desired.
    - Serve immediately or refrigerate for up to 1 hour before serving.

Enjoy your vibrant and nutritious Butternut Squash and Kale Salad!

www.ingramcontent.com/pod-product-compliance
Lightning Source LLC
LaVergne TN
LVHW081319060526
838201LV00055B/2369